Write Away!

*One Author's Favorite Activities
That Help Ordinary Writers
Become Extraordinary Writers*

Stephen Krensky

SCHOLASTIC
PROFESSIONAL **B**OOKS

NEW YORK • TORONTO • LONDON • AUCKLAND • SYDNEY

Dedication

For Natalie Babbitt,
who first guided me through the writing process.

Acknowledgments

Many thanks to Len Swanton, Nancy Wilson,
and my editor, Wendy Murray,
for their help and encouragement.

Scholastic Inc. grants teachers permission to photocopy the reproducible pages from this book for classroom use. No other part of this publication may be reproduced in whole or in part, or stored in a retrieval system, or transmitted in any form or by any means, electronic, mechanical, photocopying, recording or otherwise, without written permission of the publisher. For information regarding permission, write to Scholastic Inc., 555 Broadway, New York, NY 10012.

Cover design by Jaime Lucero
Cover illustration by Marilyn Mets
Interior design by Solutions by Design, Inc.
Interior Illustrations by Marilyn Mets

Thanks to teacher Carol Rawlings Miller for contributing "Fortune Cookie,"
"He said, She Said," and "Heated Exchange."

Thanks to teacher Jennifer Allen for her contribution to this book.

ISBN 0-590-38-208-X

TABLE OF CONTENTS

WORD CHOICE

Introduction

I love being a writer. What I can't stand is the paperwork.
—Peter De Vries

In more than 20 years as a children's book writer, I have fought fiery dragons, panned for gold with the forty-niners, befriended gentle giants, sailed across the Pacific in a dugout canoe, and interviewed the Big Bad Wolf. Though the characters and situations have often shifted dramatically, the way I write about them has always been anchored in the same writing process.

But what is this writing process? For me it is more than a simple outlet for creativity or a set of time-hardened linguistic rules. The heart of writing lies in communicating well, and doing that requires both imagination and learned skills. There are choices to be made about words, rhythm, tone, and structure, and choosing wisely among them cannot be done in an instant or a single draft.

Writing, after all, is a balancing act between the writer and the reader. On one side, you write something for your own satisfaction. On the other side, you want to share your writing effectively with your readers. So you also have to keep them in mind. This doesn't mean twisting your ideas around just to please some hypothetical audience. But it does mean explaining things clearly, focusing on the important actions and ideas, and sometimes cutting ideas (even good ones) that take away from the main thrust of the piece.

Tackling all of this can be an intimidating prospect. In my visits to schools, I often see students working hard on the "front end" of their writing—getting the ideas down on paper—but giving revision short shrift, pushing it to the side like vegetables that they eat only under protest.

For children to improve their writing ability, we need to give them the opportunity to express their talent *and* to learn how to get under the skin of writing, to find out what goes on down below.

This takes practice. Therefore, the activities included here reflect my belief that children—whether they will someday write the Great American Novel or simply compose the occasional business memo—must learn to integrate their imaginations into logical writing frameworks. There is no alchemy involved, no waving of a magic wand. Most of all, these activities are meant to underscore a central writing principle—when art and craft work together, they can create something that neither can achieve alone.

How to Use This Book

"What is the use of a book," thought Alice, *"without pictures or conversation?"*

—Lewis Carroll

With apologies to Alice, this book is a collection of activities to help children explore the writing process. This exploration has established guidelines, allowing children to be both creative and focused as they complete each assignment.

The activities themselves are organized into five sections. **Generating Ideas** activities teach students different ways to jump into writing, and provide lots of story starters to help them make the leap. The **Building Characters** section contains exercises that give students an understanding of characterization. **Elaborating** activities show students many fun ways to deepen and enliven their writing, from using weather to create a mood to using dialogue to draw readers in. The **Word Choice** section invites children to play with language. Children will see the effect of using adjectives and adverbs in their writing, and more. **Revising** activities give students entry points to effective revision, showing them how to approach organizing their writing, how to wake up stories with sensory details, and so forth. The final section, **Glossary of Literary Elements,** gives you at-a-glance definitions of terms such as *atmosphere, conflict, point of view,* and *plot.*

Each activity includes an objective, notes about what to look for in students' work, and follow-up suggestions. You can present these activities to students in sequence, or jump around to fit your ongoing curriculum needs. The important thing is to give children regular opportunities to practice and develop their writing skills. And, of course, if children manage occasionally to include pictures and conversation, Alice will be pleased.

Activities including a reproducible are marked by a ⬚ symbol.

GENERATING IDEAS

We shall probably have nothing to say, but we intend to say it at great length.

—Don Marquis

When children participate in the writing process, they use a lot of energy. Naturally, we hope to direct that energy constructively, but children must be willing partners for that. If they lack enthusiasm for the assignment, the challenge of teaching them becomes much more difficult. So the more writing approaches children learn, the more likely it becomes that they can find an appealing angle to write from. A child who does not want to write a fiction story may turn out to love reporting events in a newspaper format. A child whose imagination is unmoved by everyday events may explode with ideas in a fantasy setting. Since our overall goal is to foster each child's growth as a writer, we need first to unlock his or her interest, wherever it lies.

Often, the hardest thing about writing anything is simply getting started. Sometimes, we make this into a bigger hurdle by starting with false expectations. For example, because we read the beginning of a story first, we often assume it must be written first. This is certainly not true for me. I often jump around, writing bits and pieces from any of the four major story elements—plot, character, theme, and setting. There will be plenty of time later to sort out the pieces and put them in order.

There is also no reason for children to feel the pressure of conceiving a whole story before putting down the first word. After all, E. B. White wrote a draft of *Charlotte's Web* making no mention of Fern, who became the lead human character. And George Lucas went through several drafts of *Star Wars* before deciding that Luke Skywalker and Darth Vader were actually father and son.

Naturally, once you give children some freedom, you can expect to see a lot of different approaches. The goal is to help students get past any intimidation or nervousness so that they can concentrate on the writing itself. Whichever approach fosters that feeling in a child is a promising approach for that child to take.

Reading Between the Lines

Objective

To examine favorite stories and books to see what makes them successful

What to Do

Good reading can help create good writing. Your aspiring writers can learn about writing just from reading books, but to do that they have to look below the surface. After all, if you want to design a fast car, you can't look only at the outside of other fast cars. You have to look under the hood, examine the engine, and see how the components are put together.

So to stretch children's awareness of how the creative ideas actually fit together, have them fill out the reproducible.

What to Look For

Children's responses should go beyond saying that a book is "good" or that it had an "amazing ending." To draw out detailed responses, ask questions such as these either before you hand out the reproducible, or during a follow-up discussion: What makes a book boring? (*repetitive words, never-ending sentences, a slow story in which nothing "happens"*) What makes an ending so wonderful or so satisfying? (*when things work out for the hero or heroine the way they are meant to; when characters get what they deserve*) What makes certain scenes so vivid? (*expressive descriptions, a special rhythm, unusual punctuation*)

Follow-up

Discuss children's work on "Reading Between the Lines" and create a class list on the chalkboard of what works well and what does not in stories. Or you could approach these ideas in a different way, by having children explain what books they have found unsuccessful and why (this discussion works well at the end of the school year when they have read more works in common).

Reading Between the Lines

Choose one book to write about.
It should be a book that you liked a lot.

Name of book:

_____

Is this book fiction or nonfiction?

_____

Describe the book briefly. _____

_____

_____

How would you describe the book's mood (for example, funny, sad, suspenseful, mysterious)? Choose one or two words.

_____

What was your favorite part of the book? Why? _____

_____

Choose one sentence that describes a character very well and copy it here.

_____

What made this description special? _____

_____

_____

Find something about the writing that you didn't like (include the page number). Why didn't this part work for you?

_____

_____

The Grab Bag

Objective

To understand that a story has a plot, characters, and a setting

What to Do

When children combine story elements, they develop an appreciation for how these elements fit together.

The reproducible shows five different possibilities for each of three major story elements—plot, character, and setting. Explain each term to children. Plot will probably be the toughest for kids to grasp. Simply put, plot is what happens in the story. It's a series of events that the character is involved in, and it leads toward a dramatic climax of some kind—a conclusion.

Photocopy page 13, cut apart the boxes and place each group of five in three different containers. (Make more copies to accomodate the number of students you have). Then have students close their eyes and choose one possibility from each category. Ask them to write a short story incorporating all three elements.

What to Look For

It's quite likely that some of children's work will be pretty silly. That's okay. The important things here are to understand that creating stories involves inventing details about a person, a place, and a problem and to see if children will try to make logical connections between elements where few links are obvious. These logical connections are what make writing plausible. (For example, a U.S. president might have a funny adventure on the moon but not just because he or she happened to go there for the weekend. A more convincing scenario might involve the president giving a speech before takeoff and then accidentally getting trapped in the spaceship.)

Follow-up

Have children read their stories aloud. After the reading is over, let students discuss what they heard and suggest some rules that might generally govern story writing. Do main characters always appear at the beginning of a story, and is their early introduction a good idea? (*Usually, because readers expect to meet the main characters early. They therefore assume that any character they meet at the beginning is important. If this is not true, the reader will get confused later when the real main characters appear.*) Are some settings more mysterious than others? (*Yes. A haunted house at midnight is more spine-tingling than the local mall at noon.*) Is fantasy easier to do with people or animals? (*Both may have magic, for example, but when you use animals as characters you double the amount of fantasy since the animals usually talk, wear clothes, and so on.*)

WRITE AWAY! • GENERATING IDEAS
Scholastic Professional Books, 1998

The Grab Bag

Cut up the following story elements and divide them by group. Then have each child blindly choose one element from each group. After all children have made their selections, they should incorporate these elements into a one-or two-page story.

PLOT	CHARACTERS	SETTING
A Love Story	Children	School
A Battle	Robots	Backyard
A Missing Object	U.S. President	Ocean
A Magic Object	Monkeys	Moon
A Year-long Journey	A Bus Driver	Swamp

Scholastic Professional Books, 1998

The Grab Bag Revisited

Objective

To build on students' understanding of plot, character, and setting

What to Do

Have students rewrite their "Grab Bag" stories, keeping the characters from their first draft but selecting new situations and settings from the grab bag. Naturally, changing these elements will significantly alter their story, which will demonstrate how powerful each story element is.

What to Look For

Changing the setting and situation allows children to make the story much closer to something they might think up themselves. There are no right and wrong routes for students to take here; but to uncover elements of a successful story, you might have children read their stories aloud and then work as a class to list "Things That Work": memorable characters that are described so you can picture them, characters that are funny and make you laugh, settings you can draw a picture of, story lines that make you want to keep reading, and so on.

Follow-up

In a writer's notebook or on a sheet of paper, have children take a few minutes to jot down reflections about this activity. Did they like experimenting with the elements? Can they see how experimenting can lead to new ideas? Share that E. B. White made no mention of Fern in an early draft of *Charlotte's Web.* Did anybody discover a new idea he or she loves in the second draft? (This is a big step toward really understanding writing as an evolving process and not just a sequence of putting down the first ideas that come into one's head.)

A Perfect Match

Objective

To choose writing formats that suit writing topics

What to Do

Exposing children to an array of different writing approaches helps them pick the best format with which to express themselves.

Stories, business letters, diaries, and newspaper articles all have their own characteristics. The reproducible allows children to match different subjects to a format and explain their thinking.

What to Look For

Watch for evidence that students recognize each format and the strengths of each particular format. For example, a student might comment that a diary is one natural forum for relating the details of a family fight, because a diary is private and often kept at home.

Students should also understand that many topics lend themselves to several formats: Space aliens landing in the town square might make a strong fiction story, but it could also be presented as a newspaper article.

Follow-up

When children have finished, ask them to write a paragraph about one of the given topics. Display or read aloud the results to the class. Did students choose different ways of addressing a topic? Were different things emphasized? (*Recycling soda cans could be a business letter to a soda can or aluminum company, but it could be a newspaper article as well.*)

What I've Learned...

One reason I have written so many kinds of books is that I have come up with ideas that fit one format better than another. A good picture-book idea is not going to make a good novel. A historical topic may lend itself to a fictitious approach, or it may work better as regular nonfiction. Even easy readers like my Lionel *series, although geared for the same age group as picture books, have a particular format—short stories, cozy pictures—that is different from my picture books.*

A Perfect Match

Look at the list of writing formats:

A) diary

B) letter to a friend

C) business letter

D) newspaper article

E) fiction story

Examine the situations below. For each situation, choose the format you think would work best for writing about it and put the appropriate letter in the box. Then write the reason for the choice you made.

November 4, ...

Dear Diary,
Today at recess, this bully

☐ first day of school _____

_____

☐ argument with brother or sister _____

_____

☐ aliens landing in town square _____

_____

☐ recycling soda cans _____

_____

☐ expressing disappointment in a movie _____

_____

16

Follow the Leader

Objective

To explore how ideas can branch out in different directions

What to Do

In this activity, children continue an initial sentence with one of three courses of action. They then explain how they made their choices.

What to Look For

You're looking for children to make logical connections between the starting point and what they add to it. You don't want them arbitrarily writing whatever comes into their heads. Look for evidence that children are thinking about how actions have consequences and that these consequences will lead the story in specific ways and with varying degrees of drama.

For example, in the first scene on the reproducible, since the traveler wants to enter the castle secretly, shouting for help is not a good idea. Swimming the moat looks promising, assuming that nothing too big and hungry lives in it. Giving up and going home creates a very unsatisfying (and short) ending.

In the second situation, if Ben just closes his eyes, waiting to wake up, the story goes to sleep as fast as he does. Diving under the bed might be dangerous (if there really is a monster) or (if it simply uncovers the walkie-talkie his brother put there earlier). Calling for a parent is safe but leads either to a very short story (parent looks under the bed and finds nothing) or a story where the

parent is involved as well.

In the third scene, turning down the part in the play makes for no story at all. Getting sick and staying in bed is more of a story, but one where the focus leads away from the play. Making the best of the situation can lead to all kinds of episodes—funny, dramatic, slapstick—depending on the direction the writer chooses to take.

Follow-up

Have children tell which choice they liked least and explain what made them feel it wouldn't work. Is there anything that could make it work? What answers are most popular and why? Generally speaking, stories are successful when they unfold with action (swimming the moat) as opposed to inaction (going to sleep).

Explain to students the term *genre* and list some literary genres on the board (adventure, romance, mystery, fantasy, humor). Have students discuss these scenarios in terms of genre. Does number 1, for example, seem to be the beginning of a humorous story or an adventure story?

Follow the Leader

Look at each situation below and pick a
follow-up idea that you think will make the best
story beginning. Then explain your decision.

1. A traveler comes to a mysterious castle that she
   wishes to enter secretly. The drawbridge is up and
   the castle is surrounded by a moat. Should she . . .

   - shout for someone to lower the drawbridge?
   - swim the moat and climb the wall?
   - give up and go home?

Explain your choice. _____

_____

_____

2. Ben is lying in bed at night when he hears a voice calling his name from
   under the bed. Should he . . .

   - hope he's dreaming and wait to wake up?
   - go under the bed to see who's there?
   - shout for his parents?

Explain your choice. _____

_____

_____

3. Your teacher picks you to be the lead in the class play. Should you . . .

   - turn it down even if it means getting into trouble?
   - get sick and stay in bed until the play is over?
   - do the best you can but worry about embarrassing yourself in front of
     the whole world?

Explain your choice. _____

_____

_____

WRITE AWAY! • GENERATING IDEAS
Scholastic Professional Books, 1998

Jump Right In

Objective

To expand on story starters

What to Do

Starting a story without knowing where you're going can be a little scary. Yet many of the best stories have started with only a sentence or two and a leap of faith. To provide practice at jumping in, the reproducible lists several sentences for children to extend however they wish. As a warm-up, you may want to write a story starter of your own on the chalkboard and ask a volunteer to continue it (out loud). Encourage students to try to make their continuation on the reproducible seem as if it really fits. They should enjoy themselves here.

What to Look For

The emphasis is on getting children to recognize that although a story can expand creatively in a million directions, some directions follow more logically than others. For example, we don't know if the knight and the prince have ever met before, if they're related, if they have a score to settle, or if the knight has come to help the prince in some way. The writer is free to choose different paths for this royal pair, but each decision will narrow the future choices. If, for example, the knight and prince are friends, they cannot suddenly become enemies without a good reason.

Follow-up

Have children compare their different paragraphs. In any of the three situations, did one plot seem to be especially popular? If so, was there something about the premise that pointed more people in that direction? Did anybody try an idea that later didn't work? If so, why? Emphasize that this is fine—such discoveries are part of experimenting. Good writing involves trying things and making mistakes that you correct in revision.

If children seem enthusiastic about what they have started, have them finish these stories and share them with the class.

> ### What I've Learned...
>
> *One of the hardest things about starting to write something is that you inevitably compare it to already published books. This is very unfair. Books are so solid, so real, so professional-looking, that the few words or ideas you are thinking about always suffer by comparison. I have to remind myself that every book starts out the same way I start out—with no pictures, no hard covers, no fancy print, just an idea that the writer was willing to pursue to see what would happen.*

Jump Right In

Read the three groups of sentences below and continue the stories in any direction you like. What you add, however, must follow what came before.

1. The knight stepped out of the shadows. "I have been waiting for you a long time," he said to the prince.

_____

_____

_____

_____

_____

2. When the climbers reached the mountaintop, they found that the eagle's nest was empty.

_____

_____

_____

_____

3. Beth stood up in front of the class. Everyone was staring at her. She took a deep breath.

_____

_____

_____

_____

WRITE AWAY! • GENERATING IDEAS
Scholastic Professional Books, 1998

Story Tag

Objective

To develop story lines

What to Do

Tell students that they will each begin a story that other students will continue. They will write for five minutes. When everyone has composed a paragraph or so, they pass their paper to the right or behind them (depending on the configuration of your room), so that everyone now has someone else's beginning. Now each student will continue that story, working respectfully with its tone and themes. Encourage them to write quickly and to be spontaneous. Discourage wild changes in genre (romance turns to science fiction) or dead ends ("a bomb exploded and everyone died"). After another five minutes, ask students to pass their papers again in the same direction. Now they will be continuing the work of two other students. Repeat this four or five times, and be sure to warn students when it is time to write an ending to the story.

What to Look For

It helps for children to see that many possibilities for stories exist. Writers should never assume too much about a story beginning. They should simply follow their enthusiasm wherever it leads them. Obviously, some threads a story follows may turn out better than others. Did any of the stories seem to go off track? Perhaps, for example, one child abruptly introduced new characters or shifted the tone from suspenseful to slapstick.

Follow-up

Look at the leads (first sentences) of all the stories. As a class, decide which ones are most effective—which draw the reader in strongly. Encourage children to write riveting openers when they work on their own stories. On chart paper, have children keep a running list of the characteristics of good leads:

- ☼ They make the reader curious.
- ☼ They make the reader laugh.
- ☼ They surprise the reader.

BUILDING CHARACTERS

I start with a tingle, a kind of feeling of the story I will write. Then come the characters, and they take over, they make the story.

—Isak Dinesen

Literature is filled with memorable characters. Some of them, like Sherlock Holmes and Tom Sawyer, are so familiar that we almost forget that they never really existed. Others, like Mary Poppins and Peter Pan, radiate a kind of believability that transcends their fantastic nature.

What gives these famous figures such life and credibility? Clearly, the way they act and speak must seem very real. Their habits, their likes and dislikes, all help create an image that we eagerly accept.

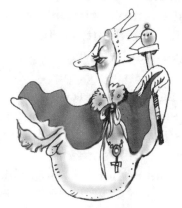

In my own books I have made up or adapted characters ranging from ordinary children to dragons to Santa Claus. In each case my goal was the same—to make each character vivid and true to itself. Identifying this goal is not the same as achieving it, but the closer a writer gets, the better he or she can hold a reader's interest through a drama, a comedy, or anything in between.

Gift Wrapped

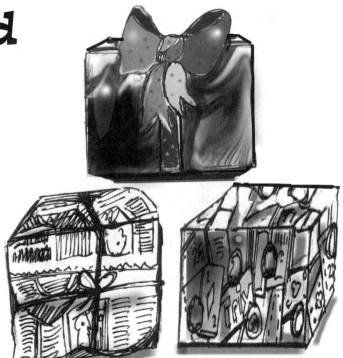

Objective

To become aware that a physical object in a story can suggest very different things about a character

What to Do

Distribute the reproducible. Ask children to write about what they think the three differently wrapped boxes hold. Then they can indicate who is giving and receiving these gifts.

What to Look For

Clearly, the distinctive wrappings described on the reproducibles may lead children in particular directions. In the first example, the yellowed paper suggests an old gift, perhaps one that was meant to be given long ago but never was. Is the recipient old as well? Was the gift discovered in an attic?

The second example is certainly zany. Is it the work of an artist, an avid recycler, or just someone with too much time on his or her hands? And who would receive such a gift? A special friend or relative? Does the wrapping include any special personal references?

The third example is the fanciest. Is it also romantic (the red bow)? Is it a gift for a very special occasion or an annual event like a birthday? Would such a wrapping best hide a cheap present, or suggest an expensive one?

Follow-up

After children have completed their writing, have them read one another's work. Did everyone feel the same way about the gifts? Give each child an envelope on which to write a new description of a gift box wrapping. The form of the wrapping should contain a clue to the gift itself. Have each child write the name of the gift on a slip of paper and put it in the envelope. Share the envelopes with the class and see if everyone working together can figure out what the gifts are.

What I've Learned...

Some people find it confining to write within guidelines. I take a different view. Instead of looking at those situations as a handicap to my imagination, I treat them as creative puzzles that need solving. The biggest such project I ever worked on was writing a children's dictionary in which every word used in a definition had to be one that the dictionary itself defined.

Gift Wrapped

Read the three descriptions of wrapped gifts below. All three gifts are wrapped in boxes that are two feet square. Based on the wrapping, write what you think is inside each box, who is giving the gift, and who is receiving it.

Gift #1 is wrapped in old, yellowed newspapers.

_____

_____

_____

_____

_____

Gift #2 is wrapped in a mixture of bottle caps, cereal boxtops, old playing cards, and supermarket coupons.

_____

_____

_____

_____

Gift #3 is wrapped in shiny gold paper with a large, red velvet bow sitting on top.

_____

_____

_____

_____

_____

First Impressions

Objective

To recognize that some types of characters have long-established traits and associations

What to Do

Explain that sometimes a character we introduce into a story already carries an impression passed along from other stories. For example, a wizard with a flowing beard is often wise, and a wolf is usually big and bad. This impression can be useful, reinforcing or helping to build the character's image,

Animal characters, in particular, often display such recognizable traits. The reproducible lists seven animals for students to identify with one descriptive word.

What to Look For

Encourage children to consider more than strictly physical attributes. For example, a skunk may be *smelly*, but it also could be *lonely* because other animals avoid it (for being smelly). Children's choices may include such descriptive words as *good, bad, clever, sneaky, smart, stupid, happy,* and *sad*. Did children find themselves influenced by real-life animal encounters or stories they had read (in, for example, *Aesop's Fables* or *Mother Goose*)? Can they remember any specific stories that showcased specific traits?

Follow-up

Can children think of any people with jobs (lawyer, firefighter, pediatrician, banker, cashier, fashion model) that have a specific reputation? Have each child write a paragraph about one such person that incorporates the traditional trait but adds a new, unexpected trait so that we see the character as an individual. Even before students start writing, encourage them to think of a name for their character and to imagine what he or she looks like.

What I've Learned...

Have you ever wondered why so many picture books or easy readers have animals as main characters? Sure, sometimes it's because authors think that animals are cute or the illustrators prefer to draw them. But there is another reason, too. Consider the Frog and Toad *or* Winnie the Pooh *books. In both cases, childlike characters have their own homes and spend their days doing what they want. If these childlike characters were actually portrayed as children, readers would be confused. Where are the parents? Why aren't these children in school? Such questions would cause a big distraction, even though nothing about the stories themselves had changed. So making those characters independent animals gave the authors much more freedom in their make-believe worlds.*

First Impressions

Many kinds of animals seem to have reputations based on how they look or act. These impressions often come from fairy tales or fables. For each of the seven animals listed here, write one word that best describes it. Then explain why you made your choice.

PIG _____

_____

_____

SHARK _____

_____

WOLF _____

_____

FOX _____

_____

SWAN _____

_____

EAGLE _____

_____

BEAR _____

_____

Name Game

Objective

To become aware that a name can help establish a character's personality

What to Do

Although names may be only a small part of any story, they can have a strong influence on a reader. Names can be more than just identifying labels; they can reveal something about a character's nature. On the reproducible, children are asked to categorize a group of names into six different categories. Remind students that there are no right and wrong answers here and that everyone's choices will be different.

What to Look For

Most likely, children will group the names similarly, given the clues contained in the names themselves. Names such as Metallik (a robot), Feather (an animal), Bayport (a town), and Brightflame (a magical creature) are physically descriptive. Discuss the characteristics of the names and how they suggest certain attributes. Mrs. Slighcarp in *The Wolves of Willoughby Chase* is indeed very sly. You may also mention that choosing a name that is the opposite of a reader's expectation can create an element of surprise. (A character can have a nice name but turn out to be nasty.)

Follow-up

Working in small groups, have children think of other categories of people and

places (aliens, teachers, imaginary countries) and come up with names for them. If they are working on their own stories, have children change some of the character names to increase their impact.

What I've Learned...

What's in a name? Quite a bit, actually. You may have noticed that in picture books or easy readers, the characters rarely have ordinary names. For example, the character from my easy reader series is named Lionel. Other popular book characters include Arthur, Henry, Lyle, Nate (the Great), Max, and (Curious) George. What do these names have in common? They are all a little distinctive or unusual.

Name Game

Place each of the listed names in the circle where you think it fits in best.

ALISON
MEENIE
BRIGHTFLAME
RUSTBUCKET
RIVERTON
BEN
HILLTOP
SPELLIA

DIGGER
METALLIK
BOLTHEAD
WEBBY
CORKSCREW
BAYPORT
BADGUY
DARKSTAR

WEEVIL
FURBALL
MICHAEL
WOODVILLE
SPARKLE
TWINKLER
FEATHER
JULIA

MAGICAL CREATURES

CHILDREN

VILLAINS

ROBOTS

ANIMALS

TOWNS

Character Stretch

Objective

To recognize how a well-defined character remains true to type, even in new situations

What to Do

Children will have fun showing how well-known characters can exist believably in new situations without changing their essential natures. As a warm-up, ask students to imagine Cinderella shopping at the village market *after* she had met her prince. How might she act? Why? (*She might be embarrassed to see the local folk now that she is a princess, or she might act ridiculously regally to prove she can do it. But in any case, she probably wouldn't be thinking twice about buying the more expensive brand of cheese!*)

What to Look For

The strongest approaches probably will be those where the original character still demonstrates his or her personality even in a new setting. For example, Santa Claus might go to Disney World, because that's a nice change from the North Pole—a warm place with many children around. Robin Hood might work in a store selling bows and arrows. The Old Woman might have lived in a crowded apartment building earlier or maybe in an open-toe sandal (where she got wet when it rained). And someone the size of Paul Bunyan might make a bicycle with two Ferris wheels.

Follow-up

After everyone has completed the activity, the class can discuss the results. Point out those scenarios that seem most in character. Then have students write a paragraph placing a well-known favorite character of theirs in a new setting.

What I've Learned...

My book The Missing Mother Goose *grew out of my realization that we know very little about some rather famous characters in children's literature. Prominent among them was Humpty Dumpty, who is initially found simply sitting on a wall. What put him there in the first place, I wondered? Did he think it was dangerous? Answering these questions led me to create a story for him and then to write stories for six other Mother Goose rhymes as well.*

Character Stretch

We associate many familiar characters with specific stories. But it's possible for those characters to jump into other situations. The characters below are just a few possibilities for you to try writing about.

Where do you think Santa Claus goes on vacation, and why does he like it there?

_____

_____

_____

_____

Robin Hood is famous for taking from the rich and giving to the poor. But what if he got a regular job instead? What do you think it would be?

_____

_____

_____

_____

"There was an old woman who lived in a shoe . . ." Where did she live before, and why do you think she found the shoe appealing?

_____

_____

_____

_____

Paul Bunyan is famous for his great size. It must have been hard for him to find any toys big enough to play with. What real-life objects do you think he would enjoy using?

_____

_____

_____

_____

Through the Ages

Objective

To explore how the passage of time can change—and not change—a character

What to Do

Ask children to invent a character and write three paragraphs about him or her. Each paragraph should come from a different period of the character's life—as a child, as middle-aged, and as old. Although the action in each paragraph naturally will be different, the character should exhibit at least one trait that does not change in all three. For example, the character might be consistently short-tempered or kind or fond of animals or a big eater.

What to Look For

The key challenge here is for children to translate one trait into three different circumstances. You can explain that a short-tempered character might throw a tantrum in his crib, quit his job in a huff, and yell at the neighbors for making too much noise. Someone who likes animals might have a favorite stuffed animal, become a veterinarian, and take in stray cats.

Follow-up

Ask children to write about how they imagine they will be as adults. What aspects of their character do they think will stay the same? Which ones will change?

Eye of the Beholder

Objective

To describe the same person from different points of view

What to Do

In this activity children will write a paragraph about the same character from two different viewpoints. Among the possibilities are:

- a spider as seen by Little Miss Muffet and by another spider

- an alien as described by a news reporter and by the alien's mother

- a baby as seen by his or her adoring mother and by the baby's rattle

- a rock star as described by his ex-wife and by one of his fans

To get children warmed up, ask a few questions that will illustrate that each one of us has a unique point of view. For example: Who likes chocolate ice cream? vanilla? strawberry? Who likes sugar cones, and who likes regular cones? You might even group students accordingly. Or have kids group themselves according to the best rock band, kind of pizza, or best song. Have them consider that if a member of each group were in a book together, these different opinions would come into play.

What to Look For

Clearly, different people will evoke different reactions. Another spider may be bored or annoyed or excited seeing a spider, whereas Little Miss Muffet obviously is frightened. A reporter will talk about an alien's "weird green hair" and the like, whereas his mom would mention "his beautiful eye and the green curls he gets from his father."

When children understand that every action or person can be looked at in different ways, they may deliberately choose more effective viewpoints in their own stories. Point out that writers of movies, books, and television shows often like to create characters who are opposites: you might call it "The Odd Couple" effect.

Follow-up

Have children write two paragraphs about an event from their own lives where their viewpoint and their parents' viewpoint were very different. The first paragraph should represent their viewpoint and the second their parents' perspective.

WRITE AWAY! • BUILDING CHARACTERS
Scholastic Professional Books, 1998

He Said, She Said

Objective

To write from the point of view of the opposite gender

What to Do

Ask students to write a one-page story from the point of view of the opposite sex and to do so as believably as possible. First, ask them what are some of the clichés about boys and girls and list these on the chalkboard. Are the clichés always true? Are they fitting some of the time? Do both sexes do everything the same, or are some things different?

What to Look For

Students often find this assignment more challenging than they anticipated. There may be a real range of responses. Don't be surprised if they resort to clichés. Ask for volunteers to read their work out loud and let the class respond to their work. Are the characters believ-able? If so, what details made them seem real? If not, why not? Did anybody have trouble writing from the point of view of the opposite sex? Ask students to reflect on why it was hard.

Follow-up

Read aloud a passage from Mark Twain's *The Adventures of Huckleberry Finn* or *Tom Sawyer* and talk about why it works as a boy's point of view. Then read aloud from Katherine Paterson's *The Great Gilly Hopkins*, and talk about why it works as a vivid characterization of a girl. In each case, what details were memorable for readers?

What I've Learned...

When I started my first book, A Big Day for Scepters *I wrote it as a first-person narrative because I thought that would be more straightforward and also an easier way to make the action seem more immediate. These are the strengths of a first-person approach. However, its biggest limitation is that you can never leave that character to get another perspective. By the end of that experience, I was so tired of being stuck with one point of view that I've never used that approach again in a chapter book.*

34

One Size Fits All

Objective

To describe an event through the eyes of different characters

What to Do

A single situation can be interpreted very differently depending on who is going through it. Have children write about the same situation through several viewpoints.

What to Look For

When matching characters and actions, children should look for natural links. For example, since billionaires are incredibly rich, a busy day might include flying all over in a private jet. On the other hand, a busy day for a beaver might mean chewing a lot of tree trunks. Indigestion for an astronaut could come from eating too much dehydrated food in space, whereas for a beaver it might involve a rotten tree trunk.

Children should compare one another's interpretations to see which ones they thought were most effective. Do not expect universal agreement. Those who want a funny tone may agree on one character, whereas those who are trying to create a mysterious or dramatic mood may choose another.

Follow-up

Have children imagine various activities through the eyes of different characters. For example, how might parents view their teenager's first time out alone with the car? How might the teenager perceive it?

One Size Fits All

Read the following paragraph:

I'm not feeling very well. I was pretty busy yesterday, Maybe I did too much. Or maybe it was something I ate. Maybe I'll lie down until I feel better.

Rewrite the paragraph to match the personalities of each character below.

An astronaut _____

_____

_____

_____

_____

A beaver _____

_____

_____

_____

A billionaire _____

_____

_____

_____

A restaurant cook _____

_____

_____

_____

WRITE AWAY! • BUILDING CHARACTERS
Scholastic Professional Books, 1998

Inside and Out

Objective
To show how psychological and physical descriptions can work together to make memorable characters

What to Do
Each child will write a short description of a character's personality (with no accompanying physical description). For example: *Alice is very nervous. She jumps at the slightest noise and is always glancing behind her. She stays out of the sunlight because she is even afraid of her own shadow.*

After everyone has written a description, partners exchange papers and write a physical description underneath the personality description already given.

What to Look For
Children can discuss whether the physical descriptions matched how they thought the character would look. It's good if the mental and physical descriptions seem connected. For example: *Alice is thin and bony because her stomach is upset so much she doesn't have much appetite. Her hair is frizzled because she is constantly running her hand through it—unless she is biting her fingernails. She doesn't sleep well, either, and she has deep circles under her eyes. In contrast to her frazzled appearance, her clothes are extremely neat from much nervous ironing.*

Follow-up
Have partners agree on a one-word description (e.g., *funny, nervous, happy, sneaky*) for a character they will make up. One student writes the physical description while the other describes the personality. Students then share the results with the class.

Food for Thought

Objective

To investigate how food can reveal a character's feelings, personality, and background

What to Do

There are many ways to show a character's emotions besides simply saying that the character is happy or sad or angry. Tell children to write a paragraph describing a character eating something. They should make the character's mood and actions while eating very clear. The character's mood will be revealed by what he or she eats and the way he or she eats it. To get kids going, share these examples: a character could juggle meatballs (showing off), twirl spaghetti like a fan (being silly), take a few bites and then stop eating (showing nervousness), or crush peanuts in a shell (showing anger). In this way the food becomes a tool revealing what the character is thinking or feeling.

What to Look For

Invite children to share their paragraphs and have the class give supportive feedback for each one. Did everyone recognize the emotion the writer was trying to convey? If not, how could the writer improve his or her piece? In general, the most successful pieces will be ones that reveal the character in a variety of ways—the choice of food, the amount of food, the mannerisms used to eat it, facial expression, and so on.

Follow-up

Ask students to reflect a little on food. Do certain foods have certain associations? How do they feel about eating ice cream? liver? turkey? Have children make a list of foods that they think could be used to reflect specific moods.

Ask children to list some of their favorite foods. Do they like to eat them at all times, or do they prefer to be in a particular mood? Do we associate certain foods with certain people? Do you assume something about someone who eats caviar for breakfast? Or chocolate cake? Or cheese and tomatoes?

WRITE AWAY! • BUILDING CHARACTERS
Scholastic Professional Books, 1998

Fortune Cookie

Objective

To explore how characters can be defined by what matters to them

What to Do

Hand out fortune cookies to students. Tell them to write a story about a character for whom the fortune means a great deal. For example, the fortune *your patience will soon be rewarded* might mean a lot to a character who has waited and wished for something for a long time. The character could be a young girl pining for a puppy, a wife waiting for her husband's return from a storm-tossed sea voyage, or a kid on tenderhooks about whether she made the softball team.

To get started, ask questions such as Who received the fortune? Was she with others or alone? What did she do after reading it? How did it relate to her life?

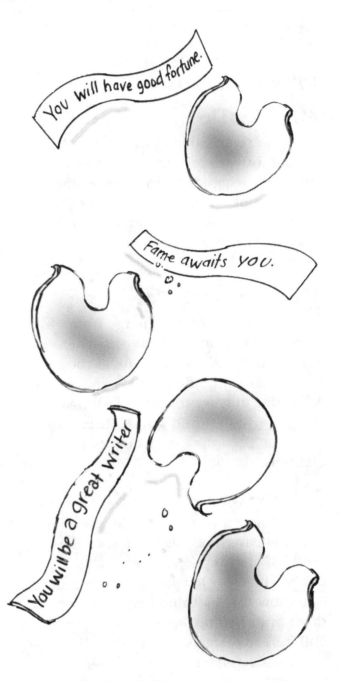

What to Look For

Students will have fun spinning their fortune stories. Look for work that truly roots the fortune in the story in an inventive way, rather than using it as an add-on to the story.

Follow-up

Hand out small strips of paper and have children write fortunes of their own. Read a few of them aloud, choose a favorite, and collaborate on a class fortune tale.

Clothes Call

Objective

To use physical details to better define story characters

What to Do

Clothes are not always mentioned in writing, but when they are, it's often only as a decorative prop. Sometimes, though, clothes can be more suggestive than that. On the reproducible, children choose clothes for characters that reinforce what they do.

What to Look For

Certain patterns may emerge from children's descriptions. Many superheroes wear tights and a cape. Lots of rock stars wear outlandish shirts and pants. A burglar may wear black clothing. Point out to children how clothes can reinforce the impression they want a character to make.

Follow-up

Have children think about kinds of professions where people wear specific kinds of clothing (e.g., firefighters, police officers, clowns, deepsea divers). Note how this clothing helps us identify them even before they speak or act. Ask children to discuss how outward appearance affects the impressions made when they meet a new person. What kinds of things can clothing suggest about a person's life?

Clothes Call

What kinds of clothing do you think each character might wear to reflect what he or she does?

CLOWN _____

_____

_____

BURGLAR _____

_____

_____

SECRET
SERVICE
AGENT _____

_____

SUPERHERO _____

_____

_____

ROCK STAR _____

_____

_____

Home Sweet Home

Objective

To help define a character through the character's environment

What to Do

Part of a character's attributes may be reflected in how and where the character lives. In this activity, students write three paragraphs describing the home of three different characters—a wizard, a pig, and a giant.

What to Look For

The key element here is making the characters' homes reflect their natures. Generic chairs or tables do not add anything to our impressions. A messy living room for the pig, though, tells us something. Or perhaps the giant has trouble getting big enough furniture (and has to sleep on three beds pushed together). And the wizard's home may be cluttered with a crystal ball or a book of spells.

Follow-up

Read aloud the passage that describes the wealthy boy's bathroom in the story "A Diamond as Big as the Ritz" by F. Scott Fitzgerald. Now invite children to write a description of a fantasy room (they may make up whatever they want).

42

ELABORATING

All the fun's in how you say a thing.

—Robert Frost

An empty house may be a well-designed and functional structure, but it is bare and unappealing compared to a fully furnished one. Stories are the same way. A writer may start with a strong idea relating to the plot or characters or an important theme, but these ideas can be improved. Often, more description, setting a mood, or creating atmosphere strengthen a story's appeal. Sometimes the trick is creating additional characters or background information. The enhancement may even be developing a different point of view for the action.

Keep this in mind when you ask students to revise their work. You might ask them to create a stronger sense of place or atmosphere or to make a scene more vivid with memorable details.

However, in the same way that a house can be decorated room by room, making creative additions is an opportunity to focus the imagination on a small section of work—a page, a paragraph, a sentence. It's important to remember, though, that a living room needs only so many couches, and a kitchen only one sink. So a writer has to experiment with these improvements, gradually learning when to add more and when enough is just right.

Mood Swings

Objective

To present the same action in different moods

What to Do

It's possible to take one action and present it with several different slants. On the reproducible, children should rewrite the paragraph to reflect a particular mood.

What to Look For

A flat piece of writing is often improved by injecting personality into it in some way—giving it an attitude, a mood. Students may give the paragraph a happy spin by writing something such as: "I can't wait for school to start because I have so many good friends I'll get to see again." A sad example might focus differently, starting "I can't believe summer is over already. It seems like it just started." An irritated mood might begin "Boy, do I hate to eat cafeteria food day after day." And a silly example might mention "wearing my clothes backward so that the teacher will tell me to leave when I'm just coming in."

Follow-up

Ask children to write about some event from their own lives, making the mood very clear through how they say things. Possibilities include being dropped off at camp, going to the dentist, shopping for school clothes, a big family dinner with lots of relatives, a sleepover at a friend's home, or taking a first roller coaster ride.

44

Mood Swings

Read the following paragraph:

It was the first day of school. I didn't want to be late, so I dressed quickly. I knew I'd be seeing some old friends in class and a lot of new kids too. My teacher has a reputation for being strict and giving a lot of homework. I don't have any big expectations for the year. I'm just going to take it one day at a time.

Choose two moods from the list below and rewrite the paragraph above in each mood.

- lonely
- irritable
- happy
- restless
- quiet
- sad
- silly

Type of approach: _____

_____

_____

_____

_____

_____

_____

Type of approach: _____

_____

_____

_____

_____

_____

_____

Look Twice

Objective

To describe the same object in different ways

What to Do

In this activity, children will write a paragraph describing a household object in two different ways. First, they describe it as briefly as possible while making clear what the object is. Second, they describe the object in as much detail as they can imagine.

What to Look For

Have children read aloud their more detailed descriptions to the class. A simple description of, say, a chair might be "a wooden seat with four legs"; whereas an embellished description of the same chair might be rendered as "carved from Black Forest oak in the Baroque style with red velvet cushion frayed at one end." A toaster can be "a small electrical appliance for toasting bread," but it also can be "a gleaming aluminum box bristling with heated coils and a spring-loaded mechanism for lifting bread up and down."

Follow-up

Drawing attention to how specific objects can be described heightens a writer's descriptive awareness. If you're working with younger students, invite them to create colored drawings of the objects they described in writing. It will show them the power their words have to paint pictures in readers' minds. Older students might enjoy looking over a favorite book to find and share a really good description with the rest of the class. You might also read to them one of your favorite descriptive passages.

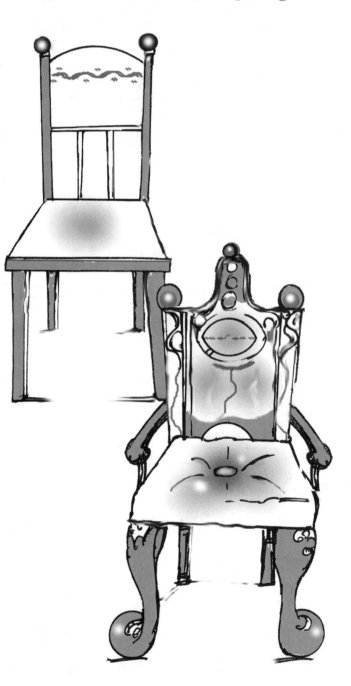

WRITE AWAY! • ELABORATING
Scholastic Professional Books, 1998

Moving On

Objective

To understand how different kinds of transportation can affect physical description

What to Do

Sometimes characters move quickly through the action, and sometimes they move slowly. How they move can affect what they see along the way and how they see it. In this activity, have children write two or three descriptions of a character crossing a landscape (mountains, forest, desert, etc.). The first time the character crosses on foot. The second time the character crosses on a bicycle. The third time the character crosses on a train. There should be no change in the action; if they are going to visit Grandma, this should remain the same in each description.

What to Look For

Since speed changes with each kind of transportation, the descriptions should also change. As the slowest mode, walking allows for seeing and recording more details. A bicycle is quicker but still allows for detailed impressions. On the train, the impression may be broader. The landscape is not so close, and it passes quickly, so the writer might mention more about what's happening in the train, not outside it.

Follow-up

In Jules Verne's *Around the World in 80 Days*, the intrepid traveler Phineas Fogg is transported in a number of ways, most famously in a balloon. You may want to suggest that children read this book (or you can read them excerpts in class) to see how different kinds of travel suggest different descriptions and emphasis.

Season's Greetings

Objective

To heighten mood through a change in seasons

What to Do

Different seasons create their own kind of moods. The same story can seem more appropriate in one season than another. Have children write a paragraph about doing something in the same place during two different seasons. Possible subjects include:

- picnicking in the park
- climbing a mountain
- watching television
- playing baseball
- gardening

What to Look For

Look for students who successfully make specific references to each season and invite them to read their paragraphs aloud. If it's summer, they might mention flowers in the park. If it's fall, they could mention leaves on the ground. Gardening would mean planting in the spring and weeding in the summer. They may deliberately avoid some seasons for some situations (like climbing a mountain in the winter). And there other things (like watching television) that don't seem season-related at all.

Follow-up

Have a class discussion of what things in students' lives are most influenced by the seasons. Answers might include

clothing, school calendars (we originally got the summers off so that children would have time to help out on their farms), and food choices. Ask them how much the weather affects their own mood. Why does it make such an impact on us?

Now ask children to review a piece of their own writing. Can they find an example where changing the season or adding a sense of seasonality could make the writing more effective? Have them try it.

What I've Learned...

I have used the difference in seasons four times to help me create books for my easy reader character, Lionel. These books used the different seasons as their foundations, and in each case I began by thinking about the seasons themselves and what makes them distinctive. I then used those features—snow in the winter or school vacation in the summer —as starting points for all of the stories in the book.

Weather or Not

Objective

To heighten the mood of a story through the weather

What to Do

Tuning in to weather and its effect on a story provides young writers with a concrete way to learn that they—as "puppeteers" of the story—can manipulate all sorts of elements to make readers feel various emotions.

Have children write a short paragraph about some outdoor activity (playing a sport, picnicking, playing ball, walking to school, riding a bike, etc.) with no mention of the weather. Now have children rewrite the paragraph, incorporating a kind of weather—sunshine, rain, or snow.

What to Look For

Ask children to work with a partner for ten minutes or so. They can take turns reading aloud their two versions and discussing them. Partners should assess whether adding the weather changes the mood. Does it make the mood more mysterious or funny or dramatic? Has the writer successfully shown the impact the weather has on the action? (That way, in a story of their own, they may decide to use weather as a descriptive tool or as a catalyst for action—like a thunderstorm ending a soccer match.)

Follow-up

Discuss the way weather is commonly used in stories. For example, characters often arrive at mysterious houses during thunderstorms, and the sun often comes out in time for happy endings. Can children think of any favorite books where weather is a factor? Older students might be interested to hear a bit from the opening of *Wuthering Heights* by Emily Bronte.

Three or four days a school year, take children outside and describe the same scene in different weather/seasons. Keep their writing in a folder. Encourage them to include how the weather makes them feel. At the end of the year, post the four samples in order around the room. Ask students to read them and react. They will be amazed at how different each version is.

Top Secret

Objective

To explore how ordinary events can be made suspenseful

What to Do

Writers can make ordinary events or actions suspenseful by adding intriguing details. Before handing out the reproducible, engage the class in this warm-up: have children decide on a mysterious premise, and write it on the chalkboard. For example: *A family arrives home one afternoon to discover a suitcase and garment bag in the middle of the living room that they've never seen before.* Now have children volunteer details that would further heighten the suspense, and write these ideas on the chalkboard (e.g., a scent of perfume in the air, a door ajar, the sound of the shower running, airline baggage tags from Seattle, a chiffon scarf trailing up the staircase, and so forth). Look at the list and then, as a class, categorize the ideas under headings such as *sound details*, *visual details*, *smell details*, and so forth. Tell children to keep these kinds of details in mind when they complete the reproducible.

What to Look For

The paragraph contains many suspense-building cues—the secretive clothing, the standing apart, the glancing at the watch. One likely direction for children to pursue is a spy scenario, but whatever they pick is fine as long as they directly connect it to the text.

Follow-up

Have children choose one ordinary daily event in their own lives (getting on the school bus home, walking in the hallway at school, eating dinner) and write about it in a way that makes it seem very important or unusual.

WRITE AWAY! • ELABORATING
Scholastic Professional Books, 1998

Top Secret

Read the following paragraph.

The figure waiting at the bus stop was hard to see in the fading light. Whoever it was had on a long raincoat, sunglasses, and a broad-brimmed hat. In one hand the figure held a leather briefcase. A few other people were waiting for the bus, but the figure stayed away from them. Every so often the figure looked at a watch and glanced around quickly.

Rewrite and develop this scene, expanding on the identity of this figure and what seems to be going on.

_____

_____

_____

_____

_____

_____

_____

_____

_____

_____

_____

_____

_____

Taking Care of Business

Objective

To use emotions to create flavor in a piece of writing

What to Do

Have children read the letter of complaint on the reproducible. Tell them that this letter did not get a response from Farmer Brown. They should rewrite the letter more strongly in order to get some satisfaction.

What to Look For

Look for student writing that conveys a clear, strong sense of emotion, such as impatience, irritation, or anger. Jack might even get threatening in his next letter. He might suggest that he will take another cow if one is not given to him. Or more comically, he could suggest sharing some of the giant beans—by dropping them on the farmer's roof. You may wish to have children work in groups to "vote" on which letters would yield a response from Farmer Brown, and which ones need to pack more of a punch.

Follow-up

Anger, of course, is only one emotional tool available to a writer. Ask children about books they have read where the characters showed strong emotion. Did those moments make them as readers feel closer to the character? What emotion do they think they would feel most comfortable writing about?

Have children pick an emotion (anger, happiness, sadness, disappoint-ment, fear, etc.) and write a scene in which that emotion is clearly present. Guide them to choose situations that match the emotion. For example, a sailor whose ship is being raided by pirates will write a frantic letter, tuck it in a bottle, and toss it in the ocean. Winning the lottery is a scenario that's ripe for an exuberant tone, while striking an apologetic note would make sense on the heels of accidentally breaking mother's favorite vase.

52

Taking Care of Business

Read the letter below.

Dear Farmer Brown,
    Do you remember me? We recently met on the road to town, and I traded my cow for a handful of your magic beans. You assured me that the beans would raise a good crop for my mother and me to eat. However, a strange thing happened. The beanstalk grew very tall overnight and has taken over our yard. Even if there are beans on the vine, they are too far up in the sky for me to reach.
    Under the circumstances, I believe you should return our cow and remove the beanstalk, too. I look forward to hearing from you.
                  Sincerely,
                  Jack

Imagine that Farmer Brown ignored this first letter. Now Jack needs to write a stronger letter to get satisfaction. How would you change the letter to make it stronger?

_____

_____

_____

_____

_____

_____

_____

_____

_____

Heated Exchange

Objective

To use dialogue effectively in a story

What to Do

Ask children to write a page of dialogue between two people who are arguing. Encourage them to give each character a very distinct way of talking—this is called the character's *voice*. For example, one character is old and has a southern accent, while the other character is young and lives in Hollywood. One character is very formal and proper, while the other fills her speech with current slang. Or one character talks very slowly, filling his speech with lots of details, while the other is to the point.

What to Look For

Students should have fun with this assignment. When they're done, have pairs read the heated dialogues aloud. Look for dialogues that worked especially well and talk about what made them effective, such as repetition of a character's language (*surely, um, you know, right*) and regionalisms.

Follow-up

Take this opportunity to introduce (or review) how to punctuate dialogue, showing students how to use opening and closing quotation marks, how to use speaker tags (*he said, she said*), how to place the comma inside the closing quotation mark, and so on. Writing incorrect samples on the chalkboard and challenging kids to fix them is always fun.

WRITE AWAY! • ELABORATING
Scholastic Professional Books, 1998

Look Who's Talking

Objective

To learn to use speaker tags to clarify dialogue

What to Do

Many writers, children and adults alike, write several lines of dialogue before identifying which character is speaking, and this can confuse the reader. Fixing this flaw is easy; it's a matter of using speaker tags—*she said, he said*, etc.—earlier in the quote. Share with children that as a rule of thumb, it's good to label a speaker no later than the first pause in the dialogue.

You may want to have children work in small groups to complete the reproducible.

What to Look For

Invite students who feel they have the hang of identifying speakers to read their work aloud. Ask: Did any one get confused? In what part of the text? Tell students that sometimes it's even better to identify the speaker *before* the speaking begins. Look at the first example where the speaker tag comes last:

> *"Wait a minute! What gives you the right to do that?" John asked, frowning.*

By the time we're told that John is speaking we may have gotten confused or perhaps already figured this out (in which case we don't need to be told). Both of these versions avoid confusion:

> *"Wait a minute!" John said, frowning. "What gives you the right to do that?"*

> *John frowned. "Wait a minute! What gives you the right to do that?"*

Follow-up

Invite children to notice how authors handle dialogue in the books they are reading. Have them look for uses of speaker tags that are new to them, flag these pages, and share them with the class.

Look Who's Talking

In each piece of dialogue below, the speaker is identified only at the end. Often readers get confused when they have to wait too long to find out who's speaking. In each example, choose an earlier point in the text to identify the speaker.

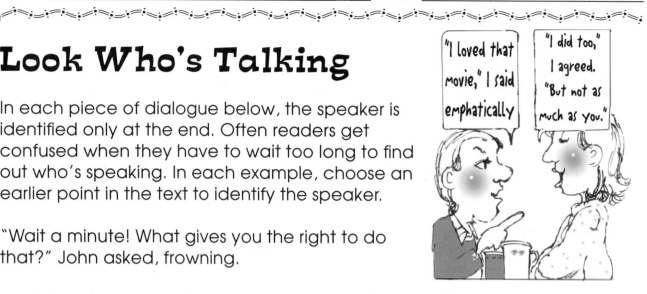

"Wait a minute! What gives you the right to do that?" John asked, frowning.

_____

_____

"Is anybody in here? Hello? I thought I heard a noise. Remember, I don't like surprises," Jennifer whispered.

_____

_____

"I know you weren't expecting me to come out on stage yet, but there was a little mix-up behind the curtain. Well, it wasn't a little mix-up exactly, it was bigger than that. Not too big, though. Well, you get the idea," said Ben.

_____

_____

"It's high up on this wall. It didn't look high from the ground, but it looks different now. Maybe I should get down," said Humpty.

_____

_____

"If we're not careful, the ship will run out of fuel before we reach the planet. I don't need to tell you what will happen to us then. Or maybe I do," the captain added.

_____

_____

WRITE AWAY! • ELABORATING
Scholastic Professional Books, 1998

Talk Is Cheap

Objective

To investigate how using or not using dialogue in a situation can influence the mood

What to Do

When people talk in a story, the reader is pulled into the action. On the other hand, sometimes you *want* the reader to stand back and get an overview of the action, so you stay with description.

In this activity, children write twice about a family dinner. In the first version, everybody should talk during the meal. In the other, the same action should proceed without dialogue. For example, one version might say, *"Please pass the potatoes," said Alex.* In the other, the same action would be written *Alex asked for the potatoes.* Children should try to make both versions as interesting as possible. Encourage them to use vivid language: for example, *Alex*

begged for the potatoes, and then heaped spoonfuls of it on his plate.

Consider breaking this activity into two different nights of homework so they can really focus on each task separately.

What to Look For

Dialogue tends to create a lively sense of immediacy, whereas description can be an effective way to show off a narrator's point of view. For example, a dinner scene described by a younger sister who is jealous of her older sister might be laced with details such as:

> *My sister Rebecca helped herself to salad. She always goes first, like she's the queen of everything. Then she passed the salad bowl around the table the other way, so I would be last to get it. She keeps bragging about how much homework she has, trying to get sympathy from Mom and Dad.*

Have students work with partners, taking turns reading aloud their two versions. Then have each student choose the version they would like to revise. Partners can give revision suggestions, using these guidelines:

- The dialogue must sound real and the speakers must be clearly identified with speaker tags.

- The description should be vivid and convey an emotion or attitude of some kind.

Follow-up

Good writers often use a *combination* of dialogue and description to tell a story. As a class, use a student's dinner dialogue and dinner description as the basis for weaving the two techniques together. So, on chart paper, show how you would write a couple of lines of dialogue about the dinner, then add a couple of lines of description, and then more dialogue. For example:

"Oh, I am *so* hungry. I had just a yogurt for lunch," my sister Rebecca said. She helped herself to the salad, like she's the queen of everything. Then she passed the salad bowl around the table the other way, so I would be last to get it. She keeps bragging about how much homework she has, trying to get sympathy from Mom and Dad.

"I can't believe I have to read a whole chapter for social studies tonight," she said, looking at my father.

"You're not the only one who has homework, you know," I said. I speared a piece of carrot and crunched it loudly. Sometimes my sister is such a show-off.

What I've Learned...

When I was writing Children of the Earth and Sky, a book about Native American tribes set in the late 1700s, I faced the problem of deciding how the characters should talk. Clearly, the rhythms and style of regular English would not accurately reflect how they actually spoke. However, even if I had known the appropriate tribal languages (which I didn't), translating them into English would still have compromised their flavor. My solution was to avoid dialogue altogether. Characters could smile or frown or jump for joy, but none of them said a word.

I expected that using this approach would be frustrating at best. Surprisingly, I changed my mind. Leaving out the dialogue gave the narrative a unique tone that I ended up thinking was well suited to the material.

Breakfast Is Served

Objective

To show that even within a short action sequence, there are many ways to create a mood

What to Do

Some kinds of actions are open to many types of mood. This reproducible presents an unspecified person who is eating breakfast. Children rewrite the scene in two out of five different genre styles—mystery, romance, fantasy, science fiction, or historical fiction.

What to Look For

For this activity to succeed, children must incorporate the flavor of the genre they've selected into their work. For example, a science fiction version might feature aliens or futuristic devices. In a historical fiction account, some reference or description would need to identify the period (the noise outside the window might be a knight on horseback). As a class or in small groups, have children read one of their paragraphs aloud without revealing the genre. Afterward, invite children to guess the genre. If it isn't clear, work together to add details that would befit the genre.

Follow-up

The book *Enchantress from the Stars* by Sylvia Louise Engdahl pulls off the trick of being several genres at once. Children might enjoy reading this book to see how the same action was described differently depending on who was interpreting it.

Breakfast Is Served

Read the following paragraph:

I entered the kitchen yawning. Wandering over to the refrigerator, I looked inside for something to eat. There wasn't much to choose from, but I took a few things. As I ate, I heard a noise outside the window. It was quiet at first, so I ignored it. But it got louder and louder. I pushed back my chair and got up to take a look.

Rewrite the paragraph two times, using two of the following five approaches:

- ☼ mystery (something odd or strange is going on)
- ☼ fantasy (containing a magical element)
- ☼ science fiction (reflecting a futuristic flavor)
- ☼ historical fiction (changing the setting to a time in the past)
- ☼ romantic fiction (creating the sense of a love story)

Type of approach: _____

_____

_____

_____

_____

_____

Type of approach: _____

_____

_____

_____

_____

_____

WRITE AWAY! • ELABORATING
Scholastic Professional Books, 1998

WORD CHOICE

The difference between the right word and the nearly right word is the same as that between lightning and the lightning bug.

—Mark Twain

Whenever you write something to share with other people, you want to avoid distracting passages, rough spots, or confusing moments that obscure your ideas. At the same time, you want to enhance or highlight those areas that will benefit from more attention.

Sometimes, with the best of intentions, we get bogged down trying to provide children with short rules—avoid the passive voice, don't split infinitives—to improve their writing, and through this they lose sight of broader guidelines. If we concentrate on getting children to develop a sense of writing rhythm and an appreciation for finding the right word or crafting the perfect phrase, they will learn more and remember what they learn. For example, if someone uses the passive voice frequently, it's not really the passive part that automatically weakens the text. Sometimes that voice may be just right. More often, it's the word repetition that bogs things down. Too many *would*s, *could*s, and *should*s can sink the most energetic idea.

So playing with language becomes an important part of the writing process. When the dust has settled on the plot and themes, it is the individual decisions about words that give the writing much of its color and texture. Like the distinctions between a house and a home, the personal touches can make all the difference.

Blast from the Past

Objective

To become aware that characters describe objects one way when the objects are familiar to them, and another when the objects are unfamiliar

What to Do

Clearly, a character's era affects his or her appreciation or understanding of certain objects. In this activity, children describe contemporary everyday objects through the eyes of a person from 1,000 years in the past. Ask them to choose the present-day objects from among the following (or offer your own):

- pencil
- portable telephone
- baseball glove
- teddy bear
- compact disc
- a school class photograph
- a Hershey's kiss
- a skateboard
- a lipstick

What to Look For

Children should have fun with this assignment. There are no right or wrong answers. If kids need ideas to get them going, share these examples: a pencil in the distant past might be described as a short spear because of its shape. A lipstick might be a paint with which to do cave paintings. A compact disc might be taken for a shiny symbol of worship.

Follow-up

Have children think about objects that might be instantly recognized in both the distant past and future. Examples might include baby toys, many foods, clothing, shoes, and chairs.

> ### What I've Learned...
> *One of the interesting things about history is how much slower things used to move. When I was writing* The Printer's Apprentice, *I was surprised to learn that technology changed at such a slow pace. The printing presses of the 1730s would have been easily recognized by Johannes Gutenberg, who invented the printing press 300 years earlier.*

Add and Subtract

Objective

*To decide which **nouns** deserve emphasis in a particular situation*

What to Do

Adding adjectives is one way to make any piece of writing more descriptive. But too much description is not a good thing. In this activity, children first add adjectives to every noun in the writing sample on the reproducible. They then rewrite, leaving in only those adjectives that they think improve the passage.

What to Look For

Some children may want to keep all the adjectives. Others may want to keep a very few. Read the different segments aloud so that children can hear how overloaded writing can get with too much description.

Follow-up

Have children create original paragraphs that they write two ways, one with every adjective possible and the other with no adjectives at all. Share the results with the class and discuss how adjectives color their writing.

What I've Learned...
When I was growing up, I definitely remember getting the impression that the best writers were the ones who used the most descriptions. This is wrong, of course, but it took me a long time to realize that I could think of myself as a writer even though my descriptions were usually brief.

Add and Subtract

Read the following passage. In each space,
add an appropriate adjective.

I have been a _____ prisoner in this

_____ dungeon for _____ months.

What _____ chance do I have for escape?

I have no _____ tools, no _____ weapons, not even a

_____ spoon to dig with. Even if I get past the _____ guards, the

_____ castle is surrounded by a _____ moat filled with

_____ creatures. Perhaps my _____ friends will come to rescue

me. It is my _____ hope.

Now that you have put an adjective everywhere possible, copy the
passage, leaving in only those adjectives that you think really improve the
writing.

_____

_____

_____

_____

_____

_____

_____

Which adjectives did you leave out and why?

_____

_____

_____

_____

WRITE AWAY! • WORD CHOICE
Scholastic Professional Books, 1998

Add and Subtract Again

Objective

To decide which verbs deserve emphasis in a particular situation

What to Do

Adding adverbs is one way to make any piece of writing more descriptive. But too much description is not a good thing. In this activity, children first add adverbs to every verb in the writing sample on the reproducible. They then rewrite the passage, leaving in only those adverbs they think improve the writing.

What to Look For

Some children may want to keep all the adverbs. Others may want to keep a very few. Read the different segments aloud so that children can hear how overloaded writing can get with too much unnecessary description.

Sometimes, too, it's better to leave out adverbs that drag down the pace. For example, *The monkeys chatter endlessly when I go by. I think they're laughing heartily at me.* The two long adverbs add a lot of syllables but not any important information. The two sentences would be better off without them.

Follow-up

Have the class stand in a circle for the ad-lib adverb game. Here's how to play: Going clockwise, turn to a student and, saying the student's name, improvise a sentence such as, *Sam looked at me and laughed merrily.* Now Sam must turn to

the student next to him and invent a sentence that uses an adverb. *Jacob smiled mischievously.* The goal is to have fun, and keep the sentences flying at a fast clip.

Add and Subtract Again

Read the passage. In each space, add an appropriate adverb.

The animals at the zoo have such different

personalities. The monkeys chatter _____

when I go by. I think they're laughing

_____ at me. The lions march _____

back and forth like they're on guard duty. The

otters are always playing _____ in the water. (I _____ wish I

could join them.) The owls sit _____ like statues, blinking. The

crocodile smiles _____ at me, but I am not fooled _____. He

is not looking _____ for a friend. He is looking _____ for

lunch.

Now that you have put an adverb everywhere possible, copy the passage,
leaving in only those adverbs that you think improve the writing.

_____

_____

_____

_____

_____

_____

_____

Which adverbs did you leave out and why?

_____

_____

WRITE AWAY! • WORD CHOICE
Scholastic Professional Books, 1998

Title Search

Objective

To consider the impact titles can have on readers

What to Do

A book's title is an introduction, an enticement, and a summing up all at the same time. On the reproducible, children write a short description of the story behind each title listed. Then they try to create another title for the story.

What to Look For

Children's story descriptions should naturally pick up on at least one key word in the title. Some of the titles are deliberately ambiguous in order to prompt varied ideas for the stories. For example, is *Dinosaurs Dance at Dawn* really about dinosaurs or about other characters who are big or in danger of extinction? Is *The Ghost in Room 5* a horror story or something funny? As for *The Big Mess*, that could be about someone's bedroom or a whole town after being hit by a hurricane.

In creating alternative titles, children need to keep in mind that titles must pique interest, spotlight the theme, or in some other appealing way refer to the story.

Follow-up

Have children make a list of three titles they liked of books they have read. What features or images made these titles so successful? Share the results with the class.

> ### What I've Learned...
> *My book* The Iron Dragon Never Sleeps *was originally called* The Railroad Summer. *My editor asked me to think up another title, one that was more suggestive of the historical tone or the book's theme of Chinese-American relations during the building of the transcontinental railroad. After some thought I came up with the new title, which I thought fit the book well but had no direct connection with it. Nowhere in the text had I referred to the train as an iron dragon. To create a bridge, I added a paragraph to the text so that the title would seem to have been taken from that spot, when the truth was the other way around.*

Title Search

Read the titles below. Write a short description
of what you think each book is about.
Then create a title of your own for the book.

The Big Mess_____

_____

_____

_____

_____

New title:_____

The Ghost in Room 5_____

_____

_____

New title:_____

Ice Scream_____

_____

_____

New title:_____

Dinosaurs Dance at Dawn_____

_____

_____

New title:_____

WRITE AWAY! • WORD CHOICE
Scholastic Professional Books, 1998

Rags to Riches

Objective

To expand the range of possibilities in making individual word choices

What to Do

Sometimes, to create a mood or effect, we need a richer word than the plain one we think of first. In this activity, children examine words and try to think of a richer substitute for each one.

What to Look For

Children should not just come up with synonyms. The idea is for them to substitute words that are more specific or focused. The following are suggested ideas:

- car/limousine
- big/enormous
- house/palace, mansion
- mean/cruel
- dirt/soil, loam, earth
- old/ancient
- smart/brilliant, brainy
- funny/hilarious
- move/walk, run, jump
- street/avenue, boulevard
- cold/chilly, frigid
- baby/infant, toddler
- try/attempt
- small/miniature, tiny

Follow-up

Ask children what effect they think changing words this way will have. Do they think they would want to heighten every word in a piece of writing or only some of them? Have children create a sentence that includes at least two of these words, once in basic form and once using the more elaborate substitutes. For example, *the small baby got cold playing in the dirt* becomes *the tiny infant got chilly playing in the soil.* Which of their sentences do children like better and why?

Rags to Riches

Look at the words below. Write another word next to each one that is a more specific, more interesting, or fancier version of the word itself.

car _____

big _____

house _____

mean _____

dirt _____   old _____

smart _____   funny _____

move _____   street _____

cold _____   baby _____

try _____   small _____

Write a sentence using a plain word. Then rewrite the sentence using the more specific word. Which sentence do you think creates a more specific, memorable picture?

_____

_____

_____

_____

_____

_____

_____

70

Riches to Rags

Objective

To choose specific, interesting words

What to Do

Sometimes, to create a mood or effect, we need a plainer word than the fancier one we think of first. In this activity, children examine words and try to think of a plainer substitute for each one.

What to Look For

Children should not just come up with synonyms. The idea is for them to substitute words that are more specific or focused. The following are suggested ideas:

- feast/meal, dinner
- demonstrate/show
- seize/take, grab
- skyscraper/building
- legend/story
- require/need
- transport/move
- remark/say
- construct/build, make
- children/kids
- numerous/many
- bolted/ran
- embraced/hugged

Follow-up

Ask children to invent and write more sentence pairs on the chalkboard and as a class, analyze these. Do they think they would want to make every word plainer in a piece of writing or only some of them?

Have children create a sentence that includes at least two specific words, Then have them dress it down with plainer substitutes. For example: *Numerous children told a legend about a mysterious feast* becomes *The group of kids told a story about a mysterious meal.* Which of their sentences do children like better and why?

Riches to Rags

Look at the words below. Write another word next to each one that is a plainer, less specific version of the word itself.

feast_____

seize_____

skyscraper_____

legend _____

transport_____

remark_____

construct _____   entire_____

children _____   numerous_____

Write a sentence using one of the plain words. Then write a sentence using a specific word. Which do you like better?

_____

_____

_____

_____

_____

_____

_____

_____

WRITE AWAY! • WORD CHOICE
Scholastic Professional Books, 1998

Stretching the Truth

Objective

To heighten or expand an action or emotion description

What to Do

Certain moments in writing benefit from more than just an ordinary description. On the reproducible, children rewrite eight ordinary sentences in a more colorful or exaggerated way.

What to Look For

This is a good opportunity for children to use their imaginations and knowledge of words. They should understand that if they go overboard with some descriptions, they can always cut them back afterward. The give-and-take of exaggeration is part of the writing process. For example, *The house was dark* becomes *It was so dark inside I couldn't see my hand waving in front of my face.*

Follow-up

Exaggerations can be fun, but they can also become too much of a good thing. Have children construct a paragraph around one of their sentences in which everything is described in a lengthy way. What do they think of this paragraph? Now have them edit the paragraph, taking away whatever exaggeration they think doesn't fit.

Stretching the Truth

Sometimes it's fun and effective to exaggerate an action or description to make it stronger. Rewrite the sentences below so that they have a more dramatic impact. Feel free to make the sentences much longer!

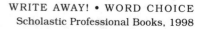

The house was dark._____

_____

_____

_____

I was feeling nervous._____

_____

_____

A storm was starting._____

_____

_____

_____

The grizzly bear made a sound. _____

_____

_____

_____

He was mad about missing the bus. _____

_____

_____

_____

WRITE AWAY! • WORD CHOICE
Scholastic Professional Books, 1998

REVISING

Your manuscript is both good and original, but the part that is good is not original and the part that is original is not good.
—Samuel Johnson

When we talk about *writing* and *revising*, we seem to imply that the first part—the writing—is somehow complete before the second part—the revising—begins. This is not true. Although a first draft of something can certainly be read from beginning to end, it is no more complete than a painting in which the painter has roughed in the main elements.

When I visit schools for writing workshops, I often find children initially claiming that their first efforts should be left alone. They don't necessarily think their work is perfect—it's just perfect enough for their purposes. Getting them to think differently demands more than our simply teaching them the rules of editing. We have to go farther and convince children of the powerful effect changes can have, so that they can see that making those changes will be worth the effort.

Wish List

Objective

To realize that the choices writers make for characters, plot, and setting in first drafts can change in later drafts

What to Do

Have children number 1 to 10 on a piece of paper. Then have them imagine ten gifts they would like to receive (toys, free pizza forever, jet planes, starring movie roles, etc.). As they imagine each wish, they should place it on the list in their order of preference. However, children are not allowed to change, erase, or swap choices once they are written down.

What to Look For

Children need to learn that their views may change as they become more familiar with a subject. Even though some children may be pretty certain about their number-one choice, picking ten things in order is hard to do. You change your mind as you go along, you forget about something until later, etc.

The same thing can happen in a story. You may start out with a few specific plot ideas or characters (like specific wishes), but you need to remain open to the possibility that the first (or second or third) order you place things in may not be the best order once you have created *all* the pieces of the story.

Follow-up

Have children look at a story they are writing with an eye to changing *one*

thing that they think could be more effective. If they have difficulty finding something that falls flat, have them show it to a partner for input. Even making small changes—such as a character's name—gives kids a sense of the power of revision.

76

Circus Acts

Objective

To think about the order of events in stories

What to Do

Even when we like all the parts of a story, it doesn't mean that those parts were necessarily presented in the most effective order. In this activity, children decide on the best order for a group of circus acts and explain how they made their decision.

What to Look For

The point here is for children to use logic in making their decisions. For example, they might split up the animal acts, thinking that too many in a row might become tedious. They may also want to choose the most exciting act (trapeze artists or being shot out of a cannon) as a climax because you don't want there to be a letdown following something really exciting (just as in a story, you want to end it quickly once the climax has been reached).

Follow-up

Have children review a story they have written. Ask them to make a list of the main things that happen. Are the events so tightly linked that their order cannot be changed? (This is good.) Are there parts of the story that can be removed and no one will notice? (This suggests that the story needs tightening.) These are the kinds of checks every writer should make when evaluating an early draft.

Circus Acts

Imagine that you are the ringmaster of a circus. It's your job to decide on the order that the acts should appear. Look at the list of acts below and number them in the order you think would be most effective for pleasing the audience. Explain your reasons in the space provided.

_____ Clown shot out of cannon

_____ Snake charmer

_____ High-wire trapeze act

_____ Trained seals balancing

_____ Lion tamer performing with lions

_____ Dancing bears

_____ Fire-eater and sword swallower

_____ March of the elephants

_____ Jugglers

_____ Clown gymnastics in the center ring

_____

_____

_____

_____

_____

_____

_____

_____

_____

_____

78

Uncommon Sense

Objective

To consider more than one of the five senses when describing a situation

What to Do

Each of the five senses—seeing, hearing, touching, smelling and tasting—provides distinct opportunities for describing or enhancing actions. While one sense may seem the logical one to focus on in a given situation, sometimes adding a second sense when you revise a piece can provide an important enhancement. For example, a rainstorm can be described with both the flash of lightning and the rumble of thunder.

On the reproducible, children are given five situations and asked to pick a second sense for describing each situation and then create a description including it.

What to Look For

Look for examples of student work that uses a second sense in a way that's detailed enough that it enhances the reader's mental picture of the scene. For example, "the fireworks sound like thunder and fall like orange flower petals" works very well, while "the bright fireworks were loud," doesn't. It's too general, even though it uses two senses.

Follow-up

Have children share their descriptions with the class. Did everyone pick the same second sense to use? Were some senses completely inappropriate (for example, taste/fireworks or smell/bad concert)? Were there any cases where one sensory description worked better than two?

Name _____ Date _____

Uncommon Sense

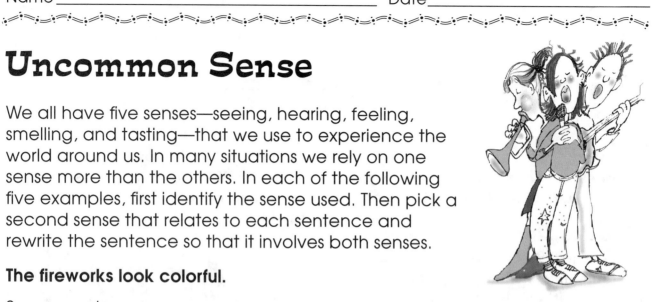

We all have five senses—seeing, hearing, feeling, smelling, and tasting—that we use to experience the world around us. In many situations we rely on one sense more than the others. In each of the following five examples, first identify the sense used. Then pick a second sense that relates to each sentence and rewrite the sentence so that it involves both senses.

The fireworks look colorful.

Sense used: _____

My new sentence: _____

_____

The band concert sounds loud.

Sense used: _____

My new sentence: _____

_____

The bakery smells sweet.

Sense used: _____

My new sentence: _____

_____

The ice cream tastes good.

Sense used: _____

My new sentence: _____

_____

The puppy feels soft.

Sense used: _____

My new sentence: _____

_____

WRITE AWAY! • REVISING
Scholastic Professional Books, 1998

Power Play

Objective

To make changes to characters after getting to know them and the story better

What to Do

Children need to understand that while creating some parts of a story it's possible to have too much of a good thing (in this case, magical powers). Have children read the reproducible and answer the questions.

What to Look For

This wizard is so powerful (an idea that might be fun to create) that there is nothing left for the story to do. Of course this is a deliberately exaggerated example, but this kind of issue comes up a lot. Children should specifically notice how the wizard's omnipotent power gets in the way of a story developing.

Follow-up

Discuss with children other kinds of ideas (too many characters, too many plots, too many themes—e.g., a story that can't decide if it's funny or sad) that might start out in a story but need to be edited out later.

Power Play

Read the following short story.

Pandrew went to see the most powerful wizard in the world. He found him in his garden. As Pandrew watched, vegetables grew and ripened on the vine in seconds.

"Hello," said Pandrew. "I've—"

The wizard nodded. "Yes, yes, I know. You want help with the dragon that's attacking your village."

"But how—?"

"I read your mind," the wizard explained. "All right, consider it done." He waved his arm. "I've sent the dragon far away. He won't bother you or anyone else again."

Pandrew was amazed. "Just like that? I thought it would take longer. Don't you need to come to our village?"

"Sorry. If you want a longer story, I can bring the dragon back."

"No, no. Thank you, I guess."

And with a quick farewell, Pandrew started for home.

Is this a good story? _____

_____

What do you like or dislike about it?_____

_____

_____

_____

How would you change it?_____

_____

_____

_____

WRITE AWAY! • REVISING
Scholastic Professional Books, 1998

Trimming the Fat

Objective

To edit out unnecessary details in dramatic action

What to Do

When students first create a story, it's natural and good to put down everything they can think of. But after a draft is complete, and they can see the plot and the characters more clearly, it's important to remove unnecessary details that drag down the narrative.

Tell students to imagine that the selection on the reproducible is a part of a just-finished draft that can now be shortened. Have them read and then rewrite it, taking out details that are in the way.

What to Look For

Although most children may agree that the excerpt needs editing, they may not all choose the same details to cut. This is because each child may see the story going in a different direction—and that direction may favor one detail over another. If, for example, there will be more about Jennifer staying up late or something with aliens, those details foreshadow the later action. If the story will never mention that stuff again, then those details are not important and should be cut.

Follow-up

Have a few students read their edited versions aloud and discuss the changes they made. What's important is for children to justify why they think one detail should stay and another one should go. Were some changes universal? Is there anything they all agree is bad? good?

Trimming the Fat

Read this short selection.

When the alarm clock went off, Jennifer groaned. Mondays were no fun at all. Part of the problem was that she had stayed up too late watching that old movie about the aliens who make a wrong turn at Saturn and end up on Earth by mistake.

Jennifer stumbled out of bed past her rug with the animals on it and her white wooden desk covered with papers. She looked in her closet for some clothes to wear. How warm was it? The blue pullover would be good, but only with a sweater. And if she did need a sweater, which one should it be? She had three favorites, especially the cable knit. She put on the radio as she got dressed.

There were more decisions to make at breakfast. She wasn't in a cereal mood, but toast seemed so . . . toastish. She had some anyway, said good-bye to her parents, who were rushing around like chickens, and went out the door. School was waiting.

What have you learned about Jennifer? Which facts or descriptions seem most important? Which facts or description would you remove? Rewrite the selection, including only the information that you think will be important to the action.

_____

_____

_____

_____

_____

_____

_____

_____

84

Plot Twists

Objective

To examine plots for distracting, unnecessary parts

What to Do

When you create a story, sometimes you put in more parts than you really need. Then you have to figure out which parts to take out. In this activity, children can add a new piece to one of the following famous stories.

- *Goldilocks and the Three Bears.* Describe what Goldilocks did from the time she woke up until she reached the bears' house.

- *Hansel and Gretel.* Add a section about how the witch moved to the forest and built her delicious house.

- *Snow White and the Seven Dwarfs.* Invent an eighth dwarf who didn't think he got enough to eat so he moved away. What was his name and why did he have problems living with the others?

What to Look For

Children have two tasks here. First, they should extend the already established stories. (Goldilocks, for example, is probably a nosy girl who is a bit too headstrong and fussy. The witch may have tried other kinds of houses first, but they never attracted any children. The eighth dwarf, Roly, left because he never got enough to eat competing with everyone else at the table.) Second, they

need to recognize that these additions, though they may be fun and interesting, don't really help the story itself and may work better as separate stories.

Follow-up

Some books have deliberately complicated plots where the complications themselves are part of the story and everything matters. Have children look at *The Westing Game* by Ellen Raskin to see just how cleverly multiple plot strands can be woven together in a single narrative.

Time Travel

Objective

To recognize that inaccurate details can detract from the power of a piece of writing

What to Do

Have children read the diary entry on the reproducible. The entry contains many anachronisms—historical impossibilities for the time indicated. Have children work in small groups to identify these anachronisms. Give them a few days to complete the assignment, so they have time to use library resources.

What to Look For

The anachronisms include:

* no alarm clocks, sandwiches, ice cream cones

* no wrist watches

* no weather reports (no radios or televisions)

Harder-to-find-anachronisms:

* no knowledge of chemistry in the 1600s to explain the connection between water and rust

* the word *traffic* was not used in that way during the period

* no forks, umbrellas, and restaurants at this time

Follow-up

Invite children to rewrite the paragraph, replacing the anachronisms with accurate historical details. They may

attempt to give the writing a period flavor by using 1600s language. For example, people were as apt to say *thee* and *thou* instead of our more modern *you*.

Many children's books are famous for being both accessible and historically accurate. Among those you may want to encourage children to read are *Johnny Tremain* by Esther Forbes, *The Midwife's Apprentice* by Karen Cushman, *The Great Brain* by John D. Fitzgerald, *Little House in the Big Woods* by Laura Ingalls Wilder, *Sarah, Plain and Tall* by Patricia MacLachlan, and *Island of the Blue Dolphins* by Scott O'Dell.

> ### What I've Learned...
> *In my easy reader* We Just Moved, *I deliberately matched modern neutral text with medieval pictures to make a funny contrast. Neither the text nor the pictures would have been as effective if they had been linked with counterparts from their own periods.*

Time Travel

Writing about different time periods requires that you create the proper mood for that era both in your plot and in its details. Keeping this in mind, how would you change the following diary entry so that it might really have been written in the 1600s?

Dear Diary,

What a day! I woke up late when my alarm clock didn't go off. On the way to the jousting match I was able to grab a quick sandwich for lunch, but I was starving by the middle of the afternoon. Luckily I bought an ice cream cone to keep my strength up until dinner. Dinner could have been better, though. I could barely get my fork into the steak because it was so tough. I considered arguing over the restaurant bill, but I decided I was too tired to bother. It started to rain on my way home, but I took out my umbrella to keep my wrist watch from getting wet. If it had ever rusted, I would've been in real trouble. I'm hoping tomorrow will be better, but the radio report mentioned more rain. Oh, well . . .

My rewrite _____

_____

_____

_____

_____

_____

_____

_____

_____

_____

LOOKING BACK

I try to leave out the parts that people skip.

—Elmore Leonard

Throughout this book I have tried to show that we should equip children with creative and practical writing tools, so they can communicate more effectively. Teaching writing, however, cannot be reduced to a few simple guidelines. It remains complicated because there is never only one road to take when developing a good idea.

The key to good writing lies in making the right choices. And the key to making the right choices is perspective. Children must learn to stand back and see clearly what will make their writing as effective as possible. They must understand that writing a story or essay is like constructing a building. During the construction process, things can get messy, and they may need to put up scaffolding, just as happens with a building. But once a building is complete, the scaffolding comes down. So, too, the written scaffolding must be removed. Students need to learn how to write a final draft, to clean up and polish and proofread their work so the beauty of what they've built—their story—can be truly appreciated.

These activities are intended to help children experiment with different writing situations and, most important, be comfortable with the idea of experimenting. My hope is that given good direction and a gentle push, children may take their writing farther than they can imagine.

Scholastic Professional Books, 1998

Glossary of Literary Elements

ATMOSPHERE

Atmosphere is the general feeling or mood in a work of literature. Writers create atmosphere by using imagery and descriptions. Readers can usually describe atmosphere in just a word or two—for example, "a *scary* poem," "an *exciting* scene," a story filled with *sadness*."

CHARACTER

A character is a person or an animal in a work of literature.

CHARACTERIZATION

Characterization is *how* the writer reveals what a character is like. Writers do this in different ways.

Direct Characterization: The writer simply tells what the character is like. Example: The goddess Aphrodite was tall, beautiful, and powerful.

Indirect Characterization: The writer gives the actual words of the character, tells what the character is thinking and feeling, tells about the character's actions, or tells how others respond to the character. Example:

> Aphrodite felt unhappy when she saw Echo crying. "I don't like to see you suffering so," the goddess said.

CLIMAX

Climax is the exciting point in the story where the main character or characters face and make a huge decision. For readers the climax is usually the most suspenseful part of the story. It's the point where the conflict will finally be settled.

CONFLICT

Conflict is the big struggle between characters or between opposing forces. A conflict may be *external* or *internal*. Some stories have both kinds of conflict.

External Conflict: The main character struggles with another person or with an outside force, like the sea.

Internal Conflict: The main chraracter struggles with opposing ideas or feelings within his or her own mind, like wanting to be independent but also needing the approval of others.

DIALOGUE

Dialogue consists of the exact words that characters say. When you write dialogue, you use quotation marks to enclose the exact words. Example:

"Don't even try to climb that mountain!" said Luis.
"Why not?" replied Shana. "I like challenges!"

IMAGERY

Imagery is language that appeals to the senses. Examples;

a freezing-cold snow cone; the fragile and gentle touch of a butterfly's wings; the screeching cry of an owl

METAPHOR

A metaphor is a word or phrase that compares one thing to another. Metaphors are not factually true, but they help readers to see events and characters in a vivid way. Example:

The hurricane was *a huge beast trying to devour us.*

MOTIVATION

Motivation is *why* characters behave in a certain way. As a reader, you can track motivation with *because* sentences. Examples:

Mafatu ventures onto the ocean alone *because* he must prove that he can be a courageous seafarer

Billie Wind sets out alone into the Everglades *because* she wants to test Seminole beliefs.

PLOT

Plot is the series of related events that make up the story. Most plots go this way:

The *introduction* tells who the main characters are and what the main conflict is.

Complications develop as characters do things to try to solve the conflict.

In the *climax* the main characters make a final decision that solves the conflict.

The story ends with a *resolution:* the writer tells what the main characters feel or do now that the conflict is over.

92

POINT OF VIEW

The point of view in a literary work is the vantage point from which the story is told. Two examples are the first-person point of view and the all-knowing point of view (third person).

SETTING

Setting is the time and place in which story events occur.

SIMILE

A simile is a figure of speech comparing two unlike things. It is often introduced by *like* or *as*. Example:

> The mountain lake is like a blue silk gown cast down upon a marble floor.

THEME

Theme is the big idea that the story conveys about life. The writer usually doesn't state the theme directly. It's up to readers to discover the theme for themselves. When you've found the theme, you'll be able to summarize it in a complete sentence or two. For example, the theme of *Call It Courage* might be "You can't be brave unless you know what it is to be afraid."

Glossary of Literary Elements is adapted from *Teaching Literary Elements* by Tara McCarthy (Scholastic Professional Books, 1997). Used by permission.

Notes